TENNESSEE
STATE PARKS BUCKET LIST

Max Kukis Galgan

ISBN: 9798758798959

Copyright © 2021

All rights reserved.

No part of this publication may be reproduced, distributed or transmitted in any form or by any means, including photocopying, recording or other electronic or mechanical methods, without the prior written permission of the publisher, except in the case of brief quotations embodied in reviews and certain other non commercial uses permitted by copyright law.

Thank you for buying my book!
I hope you like it.

Your feedback is important to me, and I would greatly appreciate it if you could take a moment to share your thoughts by leaving an online review.

Your review will not only help me improve as an author but also assist other potential readers in making informed decisions.

Once again, thank you for your support and for considering leaving a review.

Warm regards,
Max

ABOUT TENNESSEE

Tennessee, often pronounced as TEN-ih-SEE or TEN-iss-ee locally, is officially known as the State of Tennessee. It's a landlocked state located in the southeastern part of the United States. Tennessee ranks as the 36th largest state in terms of area and the 15th most populous among the 50 states. It shares borders with Kentucky to the north, Virginia to the northeast, North Carolina to the east, and Georgia, Alabama, and Mississippi to the south. To the west, it's bordered by Arkansas, and to the northwest by Missouri. Geographically, culturally, and legally, Tennessee is divided into three main regions: East, Middle, and West Tennessee. The capital and largest city of the state is Nashville, which serves as the center of its largest metropolitan area. Other significant cities in Tennessee include Memphis, Knoxville, Chattanooga, and Clarksville. As of the 2020 United States census, Tennessee had a population of approximately 6.9 million people.

The history of Tennessee is rooted in the Watauga Association, a frontier agreement established in 1772, often considered the first constitutional government west of the Appalachian Mountains. The name "Tennessee" is derived from "Tanasi," which was a Cherokee town in the eastern part of the state, pre-dating the arrival of European settlers. Initially, Tennessee was part of North Carolina, then the Southwest Territory before becoming the 16th state of the Union on June 1, 1796. It earned the nickname "The Volunteer State" due to its strong tradition of military service. During the American Civil War, Tennessee was a slave state, but it was politically divided, with the western and middle regions supporting the Confederacy and the eastern part showing pro-Union sentiments. As a result, Tennessee was the last state to secede and the first to be readmitted to the Union after the war.

In the 20th century, Tennessee shifted from being primarily agrarian to having a more diversified economy. This transformation was supported by significant federal investments, such as the Tennessee Valley Authority (TVA) and Oak Ridge, a city established during World War II for the Manhattan Project's uranium enrichment facilities. After the war, the Oak Ridge National Laboratory became a major center for scientific research. In 2016, the element "tennessine" was named in recognition of the state's contributions to its discovery, involving Oak Ridge, Vanderbilt University, and the University of Tennessee. Tennessee has also played a pivotal role in the development of various popular music genres, including country, blues, rock and roll, soul, and gospel.

The state of Tennessee boasts diverse terrain and landscapes. From east to west, it exhibits a mix of cultural characteristics from Appalachia, the Upland South, and the Deep South. The eastern border features the Blue Ridge Mountains, with some of the highest elevations in eastern North America. The Cumberland Plateau is known for its scenic valleys and waterfalls. The central region consists of cavernous bedrock and rolling hills, while West Tennessee is marked by level and fertile plains. The Tennessee River bisects the state twice, and the Mississippi River forms its western boundary. The state's economy is driven by sectors like healthcare, music, finance, automotive, chemicals, electronics, and tourism. Primary agricultural products include cattle, soybeans, corn, poultry, and cotton. Eastern Tennessee is home to the Great Smoky Mountains National Park, which is the most visited national park in the United States.

Tennessee is situated in a temperate deciduous forest biome, commonly referred to as the Eastern Deciduous Forest. It encompasses eight distinct ecoregions: the Blue Ridge, Ridge and Valley, Central Appalachian, Southwestern Appalachian, Interior Low Plateaus, Southeastern Plains, Mississippi Valley Loess Plains, and Mississippi Alluvial Plain regions. Tennessee is recognized as the most biodiverse inland state, with the Great Smoky Mountains National Park being the most biodiverse national park. Additionally, the Duck River is renowned as the most biologically diverse waterway in North America. The Nashville Basin is famous for its wide variety of plant and animal species.

Approximately 52% of Tennessee's land area is covered by forests, with oak-hickory forests being the dominant type. The state also hosts Appalachian oak-pine and cove hardwood forests in the Blue Ridge Mountains and Cumberland Plateau, along with bottomland hardwood forests that are prevalent throughout the Gulf Coastal Plain. Pine forests can be found in various areas of the state. The Southern Appalachian spruce-fir forest, located in the highest elevations of the Blue Ridge Mountains, is considered the second-most endangered ecosystem in the country. Notably, some of the last remaining large American chestnut trees grow in the Nashville Basin and are being used to develop blight-resistant trees. Middle Tennessee is home to unique and rare ecosystems known as cedar glades, which are found in areas with shallow limestone bedrock lacking overlying soil and support many plant species that are unique to these environments.

Tennessee's wildlife includes a diverse range of species, such as white-tailed deer, red and gray foxes, coyotes, raccoons, opossums, wild turkeys, rabbits, and squirrels. Black bears are native to the Blue Ridge Mountains and the Cumberland Plateau. The state boasts the third-highest number of amphibian species, with the Great Smoky Mountains being home to the most diverse salamander species in the world. Tennessee ranks second in the nation for the diversity of its freshwater fish species.

Tennessee ranks as the 11th most popular state for tourists, having welcomed a record-breaking 126 million visitors in 2019. The primary draw for tourists is the Great Smoky Mountains National Park, which stands as the most visited national park in the United States, attracting over 14 million visitors annually. This park serves as the cornerstone of a thriving tourism industry, mainly centered in the neighboring towns of Gatlinburg and Pigeon Forge. The area also features Dollywood, which is the most frequented ticketed attraction in Tennessee.

Tennessee offers a variety of attractions linked to its rich musical heritage, spread across the state. Some of the other top tourist destinations include the Tennessee State Museum and the Parthenon in Nashville, the National Civil Rights Museum and Graceland in Memphis, Lookout Mountain, the Chattanooga Choo-Choo Hotel, Ruby Falls, and the Tennessee Aquarium in Chattanooga, the American Museum of Science and Energy in Oak Ridge, the Bristol Motor Speedway, Jack Daniel's Distillery in Lynchburg, and the Hiwassee and Ocoee rivers in Polk County.

The National Park Service plays a crucial role in preserving history by maintaining four Civil War battlefields in Tennessee, namely Chickamauga and Chattanooga National Military Park, Stones River National Battlefield, Shiloh National Military Park, and Fort Donelson National Battlefield. Additionally, they operate several historical sites and trails, including Big South Fork National River and Recreation Area, Cumberland Gap National Historical Park, Overmountain Victory National Historic Trail, Trail of Tears National Historic Trail, Andrew Johnson National Historic Site, and the Manhattan Project National Historical Park.

Tennessee boasts eight National Scenic Byways, including the Natchez Trace Parkway, the East Tennessee Crossing Byway, the Great River Road, the Norris Freeway, Cumberland National Scenic Byway, Sequatchie Valley Scenic Byway, The Trace, and the Cherohala Skyway. The state also maintains 56 state parks, covering an expansive 132,000 acres. Many of these parks feature reservoirs created by TVA dams, offering a range of water-based tourist attractions.

INVENTORY

- BEAR SPRAY
- BINOCULARS
- CAMERA + ACCESSORIES
- CELL PHONE + CHARGER
- FIRST AID KIT
- FLASHLIGHT/ HEADLAMP
- FLEECE/ WATERPROOF JACKET
- GUIDE BOOK
- HAND LOTION
- HAND SANITIZER
- HIKING SHOES
- INSECT REPELLENT
- LIP BALM
- MEDICATIONS AND PAINKILLERS
- SUNGLASSES
- SNACKS
- SPARE SOCKS
- SUN HAT
- SUNSCREEN
- TOILET PAPER
- TRASH BAGS
- WALKING STICK
- WATER
- WATER SHOES/ SANDALS

PARK NAME	COUNTY	EST.	VISITED
Bicentennial Capitol Mall State Park	Davidson	1996	
Big Cypress Tree State Park	Weakley	1973	
Big Hill Pond State Park	McNairy	1977	
Big Ridge State Park	Union	1934	
Bledsoe Creek State Park	Sumner	1973	
Booker T. Washington State Park	Hamilton	1937	
Burgess Falls State Park	Putnam	1971	
Cedars of Lebanon State Park	Wilson	1937	
Chickasaw State Park	Chester	1937	
Cordell Hull Birthplace State Park	Pickett	1997	
Cove Lake State Park	Campbell	1937	
Cumberland Mountain State Park	Cumberland	1938	
Cummins Falls State Park	Jackson	2011	
David Crockett State Park	Lawrence	1959	
David Crockett Birthplace State Park	Greene	1973	
Dunbar Cave State Park	Montgomery	1973	
Edgar Evins State Park	DeKalb	1975	
Fall Creek Falls State Park	Bledsoe, Van Buren	1935	
Fort Loudoun State Historic Park	Monroe	1977	
Fort Pillow State Park	Lauderdale	1971	
Frozen Head State Park	Morgan	1970	
Harpeth River State Park	Cheatham, Davidson	1978	
Harrison Bay State Park	Hamilton	1937	
Henry Horton State Park	Marshall	1960s	
Hiwassee/Ocoee Scenic River State Park	Polk	1972	
Indian Mountain State Park	Campbell	1971	
Johnsonville State Historic Park	Humphreys	1971	
Justin P. Wilson Cumberland Trail State Park	Anderson, Bledsoe, Campbell, Claiborne, Cumberland, Hamilton, Marion, Morgan, Rhea, Scott, Sequatchie	1998	

PARK NAME	COUNTY	EST.	VISITED
Long Hunter State Park	Davidson	1978	
Meeman-Shelby Forest State Park	Shelby	1944	
Montgomery Bell State Park	Dickson	1943	
Mousetail Landing State Park	Perry	1986	
Natchez Trace State Park	Henderson	1955	
Nathan Bedford Forrest State Park	Benton	1929	
Norris Dam State Park	Anderson, Campbell	1953	
Old Stone Fort State Archaeological Park	Coffee	1973	
Panther Creek State Park	Hamblen	1967	
Paris Landing State Park	Henry	1945	
Pickett CCC Memorial State Park	Pickett	1942	
Pickwick Landing State Park	Hardin	1969	
Pinson Mounds State Archaeological Park	Madison	1966	
Port Royal State Park	Montgomery, Robertson	1978	
Radnor Lake State Park & Natural Area	Davidson	1973	
Red Clay State Park	Bradley	1979	
Reelfoot Lake State Park	Lake, Obion	1965	
Roan Mountain State Park	Carter	1959	
Rock Island State Park	Warren, White	1969	
Rocky Fork State Park	Unicoi	2012	
Seven Islands State Birding Park	Knox	2013	
Sgt. Alvin C. York State Historic Park	Fentress	1967	
South Cumberland State Park	Franklin, Grundy, Marion, Sequatchie	1978	
Standing Stone State Park	Overton	1939	
Sycamore Shoals State Historic Area	Carter	1975	
Tims Ford State Park	Franklin	1978	
T. O. Fuller State Park	Shelby	1938	
Warriors' Path State Park	Sullivan	1952	

COUNTY	PARK NAME	EST.	VISITED
Anderson, Bledsoe, Campbell, Claiborne, Cumberland, Hamilton, Marion, Morgan, Rhea, Scott, Sequatchie	Justin P. Wilson Cumberland Trail State Park	1998	
Anderson, Campbell	Norris Dam State Park	1953	
Benton	Nathan Bedford Forrest State Park	1929	
Bledsoe, Van Buren	Fall Creek Falls State Park	1935	
Bradley	Red Clay State Park	1979	
Campbell	Cove Lake State Park	1937	
Campbell	Indian Mountain State Park	1971	
Carter	Roan Mountain State Park	1959	
Carter	Sycamore Shoals State Historic Area	1975	
Cheatham, Davidson	Harpeth River State Park	1978	
Chester	Chickasaw State Park	1937	
Coffee	Old Stone Fort State Archaeological Park	1973	
Cumberland	Cumberland Mountain State Park	1938	
Davidson	Bicentennial Capitol Mall State Park	1996	
Davidson	Long Hunter State Park	1974	
Davidson	Radnor Lake State Park & Natural Area	1973	
DeKalb	Edgar Evins State Park	1975	
Dickson	Montgomery Bell State Park	1943	
Fentress	Sgt. Alvin C. York State Historic Park	1967	
Franklin	Tims Ford State Park	1978	
Franklin, Grundy, Marion, Sequatchie	South Cumberland State Park	1978	
Greene	David Crockett Birthplace State Park	1973	
Hamblen	Panther Creek State Park	1967	
Hamilton	Booker T. Washington State Park	1937	
Hamilton	Harrison Bay State Park	1937	
Hardin	Pickwick Landing State Park	1969	
Henderson	Natchez Trace State Park	1955	
Henry	Paris Landing State Park	1945	

COUNTY	PARK NAME	EST.	VISITED
Humphreys	Johnsonville State Historic Park	1971	
Jackson	Cummins Falls State Park	2011	
Knox	Seven Islands State Birding Park	2013	
Lake, Obion	Reelfoot Lake State Park	1965	
Lauderdale	Fort Pillow State Park	1971	
Lawrence	David Crockett State Park	1959	
Madison	Pinson Mounds State Archaeological Park	1966	
Marshall	Henry Horton State Park	1960s	
McNairy	Big Hill Pond State Park	1977	
Monroe	Fort Loudoun State Historic Park	1977	
Montgomery	Dunbar Cave State Park	1973	
Montgomery, Robertson	Port Royal State Park	1978	
Morgan	Frozen Head State Park	1970	
Overton	Standing Stone State Park	1939	
Perry	Mousetail Landing State Park	1986	
Pickett	Cordell Hull Birthplace State Park	1997	
Pickett	Pickett CCC Memorial State Park	1942	
Polk	Hiwassee/Ocoee Scenic River State Park	1972	
Putnam	Burgess Falls State Park	1971	
Shelby	Meeman-Shelby Forest State Park	1944	
Shelby	T. O. Fuller State Park	1938	
Sullivan	Warriors' Path State Park	1952	
Sumner	Bledsoe Creek State Park	1973	
Unicoi	Rocky Fork State Park	2012	
Union	Big Ridge State Park	1934	
Warren, White	Rock Island State Park	1969	
Weakley	Big Cypress Tree State Park	1973	
Wilson	Cedars of Lebanon State Park	1937	

1. Bicentennial Capitol Mall State Park
2. Big Cypress Tree State Park
3. Big Hill Pond State Park
4. Big Ridge State Park
5. Bledsoe Creek State Park
6. Booker T. Washington State Park
7. Burgess Falls State Park
8. Cedars of Lebanon State Park
9. Chickasaw State Park
10. Cordell Hull Birthplace State Park
11. Cove Lake State Park
12. Cumberland Mountain State Park
13. Cummins Falls State Park
14. David Crockett State Park
15. David Crockett Birthplace State Park
16. Dunbar Cave State Park
17. Edgar Evins State Park
18. Fall Creek Falls State Park
19. Fort Loudoun State Historic Park
20. Fort Pillow State Park
21. Frozen Head State Park
22. Harpeth River State Park
23. Harrison Bay State Park
24. Henry Horton State Park
25. Hiwassee/Ocoee Scenic River State Park
26. Indian Mountain State Park
27. Johnsonville State Historic Park
28. Justin P. Wilson Cumberland Trail State Park
29. Long Hunter State Park
30. Meeman-Shelby Forest State Park
31. Montgomery Bell State Park
32. Mousetail Landing State Park
33. Natchez Trace State Park
34. Nathan Bedford Forrest State Park
35. Norris Dam State Park
36. Old Stone Fort State Archaeological Park
37. Panther Creek State Park
38. Paris Landing State Park
39. Pickett CCC Memorial State Park
40. Pickwick Landing State Park
41. Pinson Mounds State Archaeological Park
42. Port Royal State Park
43. Radnor Lake State Park & Natural Area
44. Red Clay State Park
45. Reelfoot Lake State Park
46. Roan Mountain State Park
47. Rock Island State Park
48. Rocky Fork State Park
49. Seven Islands State Birding Park
50. Sgt. Alvin C. York State Historic Park
51. South Cumberland State Park
52. Standing Stone State Park
53. Sycamore Shoals State Historic Area
54. Tims Ford State Park
55. T. O. Fuller State Park
56. Warriors' Path State Park

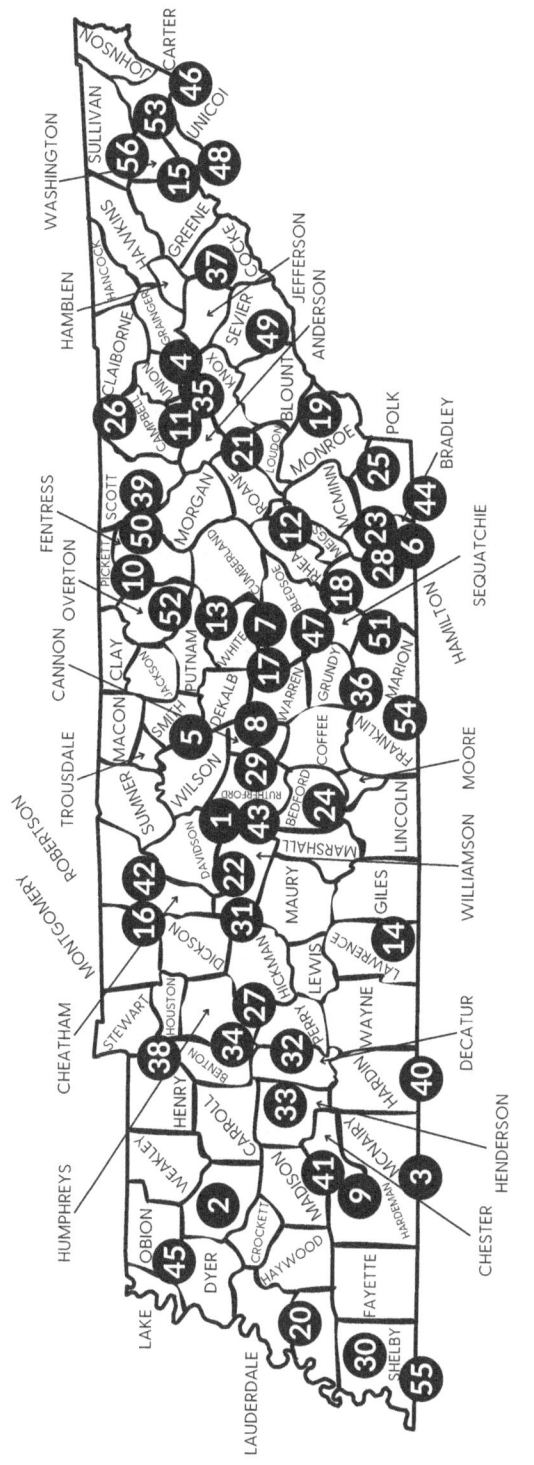

BICENTENNIAL CAPITOL MALL STATE PARK

COUNTY: DAVIDSON **ESTABLISHED:** 1996 **AREA (AC/HA):** 19 / 7,7

DATE VISITED: SPRING ☐ SUMMER ☐ FALL ☐ WINTER ☐

WEATHER: ☀ ☐ ⛅ ☐ 🌧 ☐ ❄ ☐ ⛈ ☐ 🌬 ☐ **TEMP.:**

FEE(S): **RATING:** ☆ ☆ ☆ ☆ ☆ **WILL I RETURN?** YES / NO

LODGING: **WHO I WENT WITH:**

DESCRIPTION:
The park opened to commemorate the 200th anniversary of Tennessee statehood. Visitors to the park can experience many aspects of Tennessee's history, including a 200-foot granite map of the state, a World War II memorial, a 95-Bell Carillon, a history trail and Tennessee River fountains. Eleven pots along the county walkway showcase native plant species from various regions of the state. The Bicentennial Mall includes many design elements that provide visitors with information about Tennessee's history and its natural attractions and landmarks. In 2006, the Nashville Business Journal named Bicentennial Mall the top tourist attraction in Nashville. In 2011, the American Planning Association listed the park as one of the top ten public spaces in the United States.

NOTES:

PASSPORT STAMPS

BIG CYPRESS TREE STATE PARK

COUNTY: WEAKLEY   **ESTABLISHED:** 1973   **AREA (AC/HA):** 330 / 130

DATE VISITED: SPRING ☐   SUMMER ☐   FALL ☐   WINTER ☐

WEATHER: ☀️☐ ⛅☐ 🌧️☐ ❄️☐ ⛈️☐ 🌬️☐   **TEMP.:**

FEE(S):   **RATING:** ☆ ☆ ☆ ☆ ☆   **WILL I RETURN?** YES / NO

LODGING: **WHO I WENT WITH:**

DESCRIPTION:

The park is named after a large and old bald cypress that once stood on the park grounds. The tree was about 1,350 years old when it was killed by lightning in 1976. The park is a lovely, clean and relaxing place to enjoy the purity and beauty of nature. You can see many native wildflowers and trees such as showy evening primrose, black-eyed Susans, yellow poplar, bald cypress, and dogwood. In addition to the plant life, there is an abundance of wildlife at Big Cypress, and the park is a popular spot for bird watching. Picnicking is a popular activity in the park. Wildlife includes bluebirds, doves, hawks, owls, deer, squirrels, butterflies, bats and much more.

NOTES:

PASSPORT STAMPS

BIG HILL POND STATE PARK

COUNTY: MCNAIRY **ESTABLISHED:** 1977 **AREA (AC/HA):** 4,138 / 1,675

DATE VISITED: **SPRING** ☐ **SUMMER** ☐ **FALL** ☐ **WINTER** ☐

WEATHER: ☀️☐ ⛅☐ 🌧️☐ ❄️☐ ⛈️☐ 💨☐ **TEMP.:**

FEE(S): **RATING:** ☆ ☆ ☆ ☆ ☆ **WILL I RETURN?** YES / NO

LODGING: **WHO I WENT WITH:**

DESCRIPTION:
The park is covered with deciduous forests and valleys. The central feature of the park is the 35-acre Lake Travis McNatt. The pond of the same name was created by excavation in 1853 as a pit that was the source of earth used to build a dam across the bed of the Tuscumbia and Cypress Creek for the Memphis and Charleston Railroad. In addition, the floodplain of the Tuscumbia River and Cypress Creek contains small oxbow lakes and marshes that provide desirable habitat for waterfowl, other wildlife, and fish. The park contains the Big Hill Pond fortification, which was the site of the Union defense of the Memphis and Charleston Railroad during the Civil War. Highlights of Big Hill Pond include a 70-foot observation tower that offers panoramic views of Lake Travis McNatt and a boardwalk that runs through Dismal Swamp. Visitors to Big Hill Pond State Park enjoy camping, hiking, bird watching, mountain biking, fishing and paddling on Big Hill Pond Lake in the summer. The park is home to thirty miles of night and day trails with four backpacking shelters.

NOTES:

PASSPORT STAMPS

BIG RIDGE STATE PARK

COUNTY: UNION **ESTABLISHED:** 1934 **AREA (AC/HA):** 3,687 / 1,492

DATE VISITED: SPRING ☐ SUMMER ☐ FALL ☐ WINTER ☐

WEATHER: ☀️ ☐ ☁️ ☐ 🌧️ ☐ ❄️ ☐ ⛈️ ☐ 🌬️ ☐ **TEMP.:**

FEE(S): **RATING:** ☆ ☆ ☆ ☆ ☆ **WILL I RETURN?** YES / NO

LODGING: **WHO I WENT WITH:**

DESCRIPTION:

Big Ridge State Park is lined with Early Paleozoic rocks that formed from ancient ocean sediments several hundred million years ago. The Park currently maintains a 50-site campground, 19 rustic cabins, a large group camp area, a conference room and several sports fields. The park's sandy beach, open during the summer months, is a popular swimming area. Over 15 miles of hiking trails (ranging from easy to very difficult) traverse the ridges and hollows that connect all sections of the park. Norton Gristmill is the park's most significant historic feature. The mill was built in 1825 by Tink McCoy and later purchased by Lewis Norton. The mill is now mostly a replica, although the original mill and millstones remain. Other historic features include Indian Rock, at the top of Big Ridge.

NOTES:

PASSPORT STAMPS

BLEDSOE CREEK STATE PARK

COUNTY: SUMNER   **ESTABLISHED:** 1973   **AREA (AC/HA):** 164 / 66

DATE VISITED: SPRING ☐ SUMMER ☐ FALL ☐ WINTER ☐

WEATHER: ☀️☐ ⛅☐ 🌧️☐ ❄️☐ ⛈️☐ 💨☐   **TEMP.:**

FEE(S):   **RATING:** ☆ ☆ ☆ ☆ ☆   **WILL I RETURN?** YES / NO

LODGING: **WHO I WENT WITH:**

DESCRIPTION:
The park has a rich history. It was once a prime hunting ground for the Cherokee, Creek, Shawnee and Chickamauga Indian tribes. When English settlers came to the area, the once great herds of animals were scattered and never returned. The area is home to a rich Native American history along with various historic sites nearby. The park covers much of the west bank of Bledsoe Creek at Old Hickory Lake. The park also has a designated wildlife viewing area and offers various environmental programs. More than 6 miles of hiking trails wind through the forest and along the park's shoreline. The Shoreline Trail is 4 miles long, mostly running along the lake shore and wildlife observation area. The park has a 57-site campground, two boat ramps and two picnic pavilions along with several playgrounds.

NOTES:

PASSPORT STAMPS

BOOKER T. WASHINGTON STATE PARK

COUNTY: HAMILTON   **ESTABLISHED:** 1937   **AREA (AC/HA):** 353 / 143

DATE VISITED: SPRING ☐   SUMMER ☐   FALL ☐   WINTER ☐

WEATHER: ☀☐ ☁☐ 🌧☐ ❄☐ ⛈☐ 💨☐   **TEMP.:**

FEE(S):   **RATING:** ☆ ☆ ☆ ☆ ☆   **WILL I RETURN?** YES / NO

LODGING: **WHO I WENT WITH:**

DESCRIPTION:

The park is located on the shores of Chickamauga Lake near the city of Chattanooga. It was built primarily by African American units of the Civilian Conservation Corps. The park is used by residents in many ways as it offers a number of outdoor activities, one of which is mountain biking. The park has three different bike trails to offer. Another popular recreational activity is fishing. The park is open to anglers year round with a wide variety of fish species such as largemouth bass, smallmouth bass, spotted bass, striped bass, crappie , white crappie, channel catfish, blue catfish and flathead catfish. The park is also equipped with an Olympic-sized swimming pool that includes a trampoline and a wading pool for children.

NOTES:

PASSPORT STAMPS

BURGESS FALLS STATE PARK

COUNTY: PUTNAM **ESTABLISHED:** 1971 **AREA (AC/HA):** 350 / 140

DATE VISITED: SPRING ☐ SUMMER ☐ FALL ☐ WINTER ☐

WEATHER: ☀ ☐ ⛅ ☐ 🌧 ☐ ❄ ☐ ⛈ ☐ 🌬 ☐ **TEMP.:**

FEE(S): **RATING:** ☆ ☆ ☆ ☆ ☆ **WILL I RETURN?** YES / NO

LODGING: **WHO I WENT WITH:**

DESCRIPTION:
Located on the Falling Water River, this day use park is known for its natural beauty and four waterfalls that cascade down from over 250 feet high. This area was originally inhabited by the Native American Cherokee, Creek, and Chickasaw tribes. These tribes used the land as a hunting ground until the late 1800s, when mills and sawmills began operating on the river. The Falling Water River was used to generate hydroelectric power for the city of Cookeville from 1928 to 1944. The entrance to Burgess Falls State Park is just off Tennessee State Route 135, about halfway between Cookeville and Sparta. The park is open year round, but is closed on days with heavy rainfall due to the variability of the Falling Water River.

NOTES:

PASSPORT STAMPS

CEDARS OF LEBANON STATE PARK

COUNTY: WILSON **ESTABLISHED:** 1937 **AREA (AC/HA):** 9,42 / 3,81

DATE VISITED: SPRING ☐ SUMMER ☐ FALL ☐ WINTER ☐

WEATHER: ☀☐ ⛅☐ 🌧☐ 🌨☐ ⛈☐ 🌬☐ **TEMP.:**

FEE(S): **RATING:** ☆☆☆☆☆ **WILL I RETURN?** YES / NO

LODGING: **WHO I WENT WITH:**

DESCRIPTION:

The earliest Euro-American settlers came to Wilson County in the late 1890s. The town of Lebanon, founded in 1802, was named after the abundance of red cedar in the area. In addition to red cedar, the surrounding forests include white oak and pecan. Wildlife consists mainly of rodents and birds. The park has 117 campsites, 11 picnic shelters, 8 miles of hiking trails, a group home and a conference room. A small museum, the Merritt Nature Center, displays some of the natural features of the forest. The park also has a disc golf course. Jackson Cave is one of 18 known caves located in the state forest and immediate vicinity.

NOTES:

PASSPORT STAMPS

CHICKASAW STATE PARK

COUNTY: CHESTER **ESTABLISHED:** 1937 **AREA (AC/HA):** 1,435 / 581

DATE VISITED: SPRING ☐ SUMMER ☐ FALL ☐ WINTER ☐

WEATHER: ☀️☐ ⛅☐ 🌧️☐ ❄️☐ ⛈️☐ 🌬️☐ **TEMP.:**

FEE(S): **RATING:** ☆ ☆ ☆ ☆ ☆ **WILL I RETURN?** YES / NO

LODGING: **WHO I WENT WITH:**

DESCRIPTION:
Chickasaw State Park is named after the Chickasaw Indians who once inhabited western Tennessee and northern Mississippi. The park offers many activities to its visitors including camping, golfing, paddle boarding, bird watching, swimming, hiking, biking, fishing and horseback riding. Guests can rent paddle boats and pedal boats on Lake Placid. There are eight hiking trails in the park. Chickasaw has three campgrounds: the RV campground, the tent campground, and the wrangler campground.

NOTES:

PASSPORT STAMPS

CORDELL HULL BIRTHPLACE STATE PARK

COUNTY: PICKETT   **ESTABLISHED:** 1997   **AREA (AC/HA):** 58 / 23

DATE VISITED: SPRING ☐   SUMMER ☐   FALL ☐   WINTER ☐

WEATHER: ☀ ☐ ☁ ☐ 🌧 ☐ ❄ ☐ ⛈ ☐ 🌬 ☐   **TEMP.:**

FEE(S):   **RATING:** ☆ ☆ ☆ ☆ ☆   **WILL I RETURN?**   YES / NO

LODGING: **WHO I WENT WITH:**

DESCRIPTION:

Cordell Hull was U.S. Secretary of State under President Franklin Roosevelt and played a key role in the creation of the United Nations in the mid-1940s. The park includes a library that houses the entire Cordell Hull collection of more than 1,500 books and hundreds of original photographs, documents and three-dimensional objects. The collection includes a replica of his Nobel Peace Prize. The park is located along the Highland Rim, an arid and hilly area. One of the many notable caves located on the limestone-rich Highlands Rim is Bunkum Cave, which is located along the upper reaches of Gulf Cove, just south of Cordell Hull's birthplace. Currently, a permit is required to visit the cave outside of its lighted area.

NOTES:

PASSPORT STAMPS

COVE LAKE STATE PARK

COUNTY: CAMPBELL   **ESTABLISHED:** 1937   **AREA (AC/HA):** 673 / 272

DATE VISITED: **SPRING** ☐   **SUMMER** ☐   **FALL** ☐   **WINTER** ☐

WEATHER: ☀️☐ ⛅☐ 🌧️☐ ❄️☐ ⛈️☐ 🌬️☐   **TEMP.:**

FEE(S):   **RATING:** ☆ ☆ ☆ ☆ ☆   **WILL I RETURN?** YES / NO

LODGING: **WHO I WENT WITH:**

DESCRIPTION:
The park is located in a beautiful mountain valley on the eastern edge of the Cumberland Plateau. The park is located around Cove Lake, a damming of Cove Creek created by the completion of Caryville Dam in 1936. Picturesque nature trails lead through a variety of wetlands and woodlands, offering wildlife viewing for nature lovers. A paved walking/biking trail provides easy access to all park facilities. The park has a large campground, several small hiking trails and a wildlife viewing area. Several small hiking trails wind through the park, including a 3.5-mile paved trail that runs along the lake shore and a trail that provides access to Wheeler Cemetery and Caryville Dam. The park's wildlife observation area is located in the northwest corner of the park and includes a 15-foot observation tower.

NOTES:

PASSPORT STAMPS

CUMBERLAND MOUNTAIN STATE PARK

COUNTY: CUMBERLAND **ESTABLISHED:** 1938 **AREA (AC/HA):** 1,720 / 700

DATE VISITED: SPRING ☐ SUMMER ☐ FALL ☐ WINTER ☐

WEATHER: ☀ ☐ ⛅ ☐ 🌧 ☐ 🌨 ☐ ⛈ ☐ 🌬 ☐ **TEMP.:**

FEE(S): **RATING:** ☆ ☆ ☆ ☆ ☆ **WILL I RETURN?** YES / NO

LODGING: **WHO I WENT WITH:**

DESCRIPTION:

The park is located around Byrd Lake, an artificial lake created by damming Byrd Creek in the 1930s. It provides numerous recreational activities, including an 18-hole Bear Trace golf course. Recreational facilities include an Olympic-size swimming pool, picnic pavilions, playgrounds, four tennis courts, and shuffleboard, basketball, badminton and volleyball courts. Several miles of hiking trails wind through the park, primarily along Byrd Creek and the adjacent hills. The Cumberland Homesteads Tower Museum, located 1 mile from the park, recalls the development of the Cumberland Homestead Community of the 1930s.

NOTES:

PASSPORT STAMPS

CUMMINS FALLS STATE PARK

COUNTY: JACKSON　　　**ESTABLISHED:** 2011　　　**AREA (AC/HA):** 211 / 85

DATE VISITED:　　　　　　　　　SPRING ☐　SUMMER ☐　FALL ☐　WINTER ☐

WEATHER: ☀ ☐　⛅ ☐　🌧 ☐　❄ ☐　⛈ ☐　🌬 ☐　**TEMP.:**

FEE(S):　　　　**RATING:** ☆ ☆ ☆ ☆ ☆　　　**WILL I RETURN?** YES / NO

LODGING:　　　　　　　**WHO I WENT WITH:**

DESCRIPTION:
Park located northwest of Cookeville. Its namesake, Cummins Falls, is a 75-foot waterfall that sits on the scenic Blackburn Fork State Scenic River. The park was purchased and created by the Tennessee Parks and Greenways Foundation in 2011. The park offers picnicking, hiking and fishing. Cummins Falls is the eighth largest waterfall in Tennessee by volume of water and is 75 feet high.

NOTES:

PASSPORT STAMPS

DAVID CROCKETT STATE PARK

COUNTY: LAWRENCE **ESTABLISHED:** 1959 **AREA (AC/HA):** 1,100 / 450

DATE VISITED: SPRING ☐ SUMMER ☐ FALL ☐ WINTER ☐

WEATHER: ☀ ☐ ☁ ☐ 🌧 ☐ ❄ ☐ ⛈ ☐ 💨 ☐ **TEMP.:**

FEE(S): **RATING:** ☆ ☆ ☆ ☆ ☆ **WILL I RETURN?** YES / NO

LODGING: **WHO I WENT WITH:**

DESCRIPTION:

David Crockett was a pioneer, soldier, politician and industrialist. He was born in 1786 near the small town of Limestone in northeast Tennessee. He moved to Lawrence County in 1817 and served as a justice of the peace, militia colonel, and state representative. Along the banks of Shoal Creek, he established a diversified industry consisting of a powder mill, a mill, and a distillery at the site that is now his namesake. The park features a museum with exhibits depicting Crockett's life and a water-powered grist mill. The 40-acre lake offers fishing and boating opportunities.

NOTES:

PASSPORT STAMPS

DAVID CROCKETT BIRTHPLACE STATE PARK

COUNTY: GREENE **ESTABLISHED:** 1973 **AREA (AC/HA):** 105 / 42

DATE VISITED: SPRING ☐ SUMMER ☐ FALL ☐ WINTER ☐

WEATHER: ☀☐ ⛅☐ 🌧☐ ❄☐ ⛈☐ 🌬☐ **TEMP.:**

FEE(S): **RATING:** ☆ ☆ ☆ ☆ ☆ **WILL I RETURN?** YES / NO

LODGING: **WHO I WENT WITH:**

DESCRIPTION:
The park has a visitor center, 88 campsites, 2 picnic pavilions, 2 picnic areas, a swimming pool, a playground and a public boat launch ramp. Several short hiking trails lead along the riverbank and bluffs. The park has 80+ campsites, 40 of which are fully equipped. This park has a replica cabin and also has an 18th century farmstead. The park also has opportunities for bass-fishing and other types of fishing.

NOTES:

PASSPORT STAMPS

DUNBAR CAVE STATE PARK

COUNTY: MONTGOMERY **ESTABLISHED:** 1973 **AREA (AC/HA):** 110 / 45

DATE VISITED: SPRING ☐ SUMMER ☐ FALL ☐ WINTER ☐

WEATHER: ☀ ☐ ⛅ ☐ 🌧 ☐ ❄ ☐ ⛈ ☐ 🌬 ☐ **TEMP.:**

FEE(S): **RATING:** ☆ ☆ ☆ ☆ ☆ **WILL I RETURN?** YES / NO

LODGING: **WHO I WENT WITH:**

DESCRIPTION:

Dunbar Cave is the 280th largest cave complex in the world, stretching 13 km inward. The cave is located in a karst area, including sinkholes, springs and limestone bedrock. In front of the cave entrance is a large concrete structure with three distinct arches and an artificial swan lake. Dunbar Cave has a small bat population and is closed from September to April to allow the bats to hibernate undisturbed. Over 30 drawings and etchings found in the cave have been dated to the Mississippian era (700 to 1300 AD) using torches and other artifacts found nearby. Some of the pictographs are religious symbols, one of which depicts a supernatural Mississippian warrior.

NOTES:

PASSPORT STAMPS

EDGAR EVINS STATE PARK

COUNTY: DEKALB   **ESTABLISHED:** 1975   **AREA (AC/HA):** 6,000 / 2,400

DATE VISITED: SPRING ☐   SUMMER ☐   FALL ☐   WINTER ☐

WEATHER: ☀️☐ ⛅☐ 🌧️☐ ❄️☐ ⛈️☐ 🌬️☐   **TEMP.:**

FEE(S):   **RATING:** ☆ ☆ ☆ ☆ ☆   **WILL I RETURN?** YES / NO

LODGING: **WHO I WENT WITH:**

DESCRIPTION:

James Edgar Evins (1883-1954), the park's namesake, was a Smithville businessman, mayor and state senator who was instrumental in the development of Centre Hill Dam and Reservoir in the 1940s. The park is located on the shores of Centre Hill Lake on the steep, hilly terrain of the Eastern Highland Rim. Most of the Park is covered with deciduous forest, typical of the Eastern Highland Rim. Common tree species include the tuliptree, white basswood, sugar maple, white ash, and various species of oak and hickory. Wooden platforms, reinforced with concrete and steel around the slopes of Centre Hill Lake, are a unique feature of the 60 campsites available at Edgar Evins State Park. Plenty of wildlife can be found in this park, including several rare birds. Wildlife is abundant and includes three different species of owls, numerous hawks and wintering white-tailed eagles, and the rare aquatic warbler. There is a marina and restaurant on the lake, and the park has a gift store.

NOTES:

PASSPORT STAMPS

FALL CREEK FALLS STATE PARK

COUNTY: VAN BUREN, BLEDSOE   **ESTABLISHED:** 1935   **AREA (AC/HA):** 26,000 / 11,000

DATE VISITED: SPRING ☐   SUMMER ☐   FALL ☐   WINTER ☐

WEATHER: ☀☐ ⛅☐ 🌧☐ ❄☐ ⛈☐ 🌫☐   **TEMP.:**

FEE(S):   **RATING:** ☆ ☆ ☆ ☆ ☆   **WILL I RETURN?**   YES / NO

LODGING: **WHO I WENT WITH:**

DESCRIPTION:

The park focuses on the upper Cane Creek Gorge, an area known for its unique geologic formations and scenic waterfalls. The park's namesake is 256-foot Fall Creek Falls, the highest free-fall waterfall east of the Mississippi River. Fall Creek Falls artificial lake, controlled by a dam, provides a continuous flow of water to Fall Creek Falls. The lake dominates the southern portion of the park. The park has many activities suitable for visitors of all ages and skill levels. Hikers can choose short or long walks around the lake and to the base of Fall Creek Falls. There are two long-distance night trails for adventure-seeking hikers, while day trails are designed to accommodate recreational and educational activities for all ages. You can explore over 56 miles of trails. The park offers an 18-hole golf course, an Olympic-sized swimming pool and several paved bike trails.

NOTES:

PASSPORT STAMPS

FORT LOUDOUN STATE HISTORIC PARK

COUNTY: MONROE   ESTABLISHED: 1977   AREA (AC/HA): 1,200 / 490

DATE VISITED: SPRING ☐ SUMMER ☐ FALL ☐ WINTER ☐

WEATHER: ☀☐ ⛅☐ 🌧☐ ❄☐ ⛈☐ 🌬☐   TEMP.:

FEE(S):   RATING: ☆ ☆ ☆ ☆ ☆   WILL I RETURN? YES / NO

LODGING: WHO I WENT WITH:

DESCRIPTION:
The park is one of the earliest British fortifications on the western frontier, built in 1756. The fort was reconstructed during the Great Depression. There are three hiking trails in the park, ranging from easy to moderately challenging. The trails are for day use only. The trails are the Ridgetop Loop Trail, which is about 1.5 miles long and provides beautiful views of the mountains and valley; the Meadow Loop Trail, which is about 2.25 miles long; and the Lost Shoe Loop, which is about 0.5 miles long. Fishing is available at Tellico Lake Park. There are multiple boat ramps and marinas serving the Tellico Lake area. There are many options for shore or boat fishing. At the picnic area, guests will find a handicap accessible pier large enough to accommodate many anglers. During garrison weekends there are demonstrations: artillery and musketry, ambulatory, blacksmithing, woodworking, laundry and leatherworking.

NOTES:

PASSPORT STAMPS

FORT PILLOW STATE PARK

COUNTY: LAUDERDALE **ESTABLISHED:** 1971 **AREA (AC/HA):** 1,642 / 664

DATE VISITED: SPRING ☐ SUMMER ☐ FALL ☐ WINTER ☐

WEATHER: ☀ ☐ ⛅ ☐ 🌧 ☐ ❄ ☐ ⛈ ☐ 🌬 ☐ **TEMP.:**

FEE(S): **RATING:** ☆ ☆ ☆ ☆ ☆ **WILL I RETURN?** YES / NO

LODGING: **WHO I WENT WITH:**

DESCRIPTION:

The park preserves the site of the battle of Fort Pillow after the Civil War. Fort Pillow is located on the bluffs of Chickasaw Bluff overlooking the Mississippi River and is rich in both history and archaeology. The park includes an interpretive center and museum. Tours of the museum and restored fortifications are available upon request. The park's museum offers Civil War artifacts, including a cannon and interpretive displays related to the history of Fort Pillow. The park also offers many recreational activities, including camping, picnicking, and fishing. The park was designated as a Wildlife Observation Area by the Tennessee Wildlife Resources Agency and is frequented by bird watchers.

NOTES:

PASSPORT STAMPS

FROZEN HEAD STATE PARK

COUNTY: MORGAN   **ESTABLISHED:** 1970   **AREA (AC/HA):** 24,000 / 9,700

DATE VISITED: SPRING ☐ SUMMER ☐ FALL ☐ WINTER ☐

WEATHER: ☀☐ ⛅☐ 🌧☐ ❄☐ ⛈☐ 💨☐   **TEMP.:**

FEE(S):   **RATING:** ☆ ☆ ☆ ☆ ☆   **WILL I RETURN?** YES / NO

LODGING: **WHO I WENT WITH:**

DESCRIPTION:
The park is named after a 3,324-foot peak in the Cumberland Mountains whose summit is often covered in ice or snow during the winter months. There are 20 tent campsites within the park. Fifty miles of hiking and backpacking trails provide wildlife viewing opportunities. Most trails are open to hiking only, although mountain biking is allowed on the Lookout Tower Trail, which leads to the top of Frozen Head. The Barkley Marathons is an unusual ultramarathon event that has been held annually in the park since 1984. Competitors are challenged to run a 100-mile course in under 60 hours. The course is unmarked and traverses very rugged and brushy terrain. As of 2021, only fifteen competitors have ever finished the race.

NOTES:

PASSPORT STAMPS

HARPETH RIVER STATE PARK

COUNTY: CHEATHAM, DAVIDSON **ESTABLISHED:** 1978 **AREA (AC/HA):** 520 / 210

DATE VISITED: SPRING ☐   SUMMER ☐   FALL ☐   WINTER ☐

WEATHER: ☀ ☐   ☁ ☐   🌧 ☐   ❄ ☐   ⛈ ☐   🌬 ☐   **TEMP.:**

FEE(S):   **RATING:** ☆ ☆ ☆ ☆ ☆   **WILL I RETURN?**   YES / NO

LODGING: **WHO I WENT WITH:**

DESCRIPTION:

The park is a linear park (extending 40 miles of river) that was created to connect several state historic, natural, and archaeological sites along the lower Harpeth River. The park is popular for kayaking, fishing, and hiking. Canoeing is available for beginners and advanced paddlers with access points located at all sites within the park (except archaeological sites). For hikers and nature lovers, the park offers lush forests, majestic bluffs, and flourishing field meadows. Visitors can also enjoy the park's picnic areas.

NOTES:

PASSPORT STAMPS

HARRISON BAY STATE PARK

COUNTY: HAMILTON **ESTABLISHED:** 1937 **AREA (AC/HA):** 1,200 / 490

DATE VISITED: SPRING ☐ SUMMER ☐ FALL ☐ WINTER ☐

WEATHER: ☀☐ ☁☐ 🌧☐ ❄☐ ⛈☐ 🌬☐ **TEMP.:**

FEE(S): **RATING:** ☆ ☆ ☆ ☆ ☆ **WILL I RETURN?** YES / NO

LODGING: **WHO I WENT WITH:**

DESCRIPTION:
The park is named for the large bay on the main channel of the Tennessee River that includes the old town of Harrison and the last Cherokee campground. This beautiful wooded park is a haven for campers, golfers, boaters and fishermen, as well as picnickers and other visitors. The park offers a 4.5-mile loop bike trail. This trail features pleasant uphill climbs and some fast descents. The trail is fun and designed for all abilities.

NOTES:

PASSPORT STAMPS

HENRY HORTON STATE PARK

COUNTY: MARSHALL **ESTABLISHED:** 1960s **AREA (AC/HA):** 1,523 / 616

DATE VISITED: SPRING ☐ SUMMER ☐ FALL ☐ WINTER ☐

WEATHER: ☀ ☐ ⛅ ☐ 🌧 ☐ ❄ ☐ ⛈ ☐ 🌬 ☐ **TEMP.:**

FEE(S): **RATING:** ☆ ☆ ☆ ☆ ☆ **WILL I RETURN?** YES / NO

LODGING: **WHO I WENT WITH:**

DESCRIPTION:

The park was created in the 1960s on the estate of former Tennessee Governor Henry Horton. The park is located on the banks of the historic Duck River, one of the most diverse ecosystems in the world. Remnants of a mill and bridge operated and used by Horton's wife's family for over a century can be seen today on the Wilhoite Mill Trail. The park offers canoeing, golfing, biking, camping and hiking. Henry Horton offers 75 campsites located near the scenic Duck River. There are four relatively flat, easy hiking trails in the park, some overlooking the Duck River. Facilities for baseball, basketball, tennis and volleyball are available.

NOTES:

PASSPORT STAMPS

HIWASSEE/OCOEE SCENIC RIVER STATE PARK

COUNTY: POLK   **ESTABLISHED:** 1972   **AREA (AC/HA):** - / -

DATE VISITED: SPRING ☐   SUMMER ☐   FALL ☐   WINTER ☐

WEATHER: ☀ ☐ ⛅ ☐ 🌧 ☐ ❄ ☐ ⛈ ☐ 🌬 ☐   **TEMP.:**

FEE(S):   **RATING:** ☆ ☆ ☆ ☆   **WILL I RETURN?** YES / NO

LODGING: **WHO I WENT WITH:**

DESCRIPTION:

Hiwassee/Ocoee Scenic River State Park was the first river included in the State Scenic River Program. The 23 river mile stretch from North Carolina to U.S. Hwy. 411 north of Benton, was designated as a Class III, partially developed river. Swimming, canoeing, and rafting are major attractions of both the Hiwassee and Ocoee Rivers. Numerous public sites provide boat launch ramps. The park is also a popular fishing stream, and anglers of all ages can catch largemouth bass, yellow perch, catfish, and brook and rainbow trout.

NOTES:

PASSPORT STAMPS

INDIAN MOUNTAIN STATE PARK

COUNTY: CAMPBELL   **ESTABLISHED:** 1971   **AREA (AC/HA):** 213 / 86

DATE VISITED: SPRING ☐   SUMMER ☐   FALL ☐   WINTER ☐

WEATHER: ☀ ☐   ⛅ ☐   🌧 ☐   ❄ ☐   ⛈ ☐   🌬 ☐   **TEMP.:**

FEE(S):   **RATING:** ☆ ☆ ☆ ☆ ☆   **WILL I RETURN?** YES / NO

LODGING: **WHO I WENT WITH:**

DESCRIPTION:

The city of Jellico originally acquired the park in the late 1960s through a federal open space grant under provisions of the 1961 Federal Housing Act. Park visitors can fish in the lake, picnic, camp and hike on three trails. Two official hiking trails wind along both sides of Elk Creek. Water bikes are available for rent at Indian Mountain Lake. Several sports fields are located along London Avenue in the northeastern part of the park. A third half-mile unmarked trail surrounds a pond in the southeastern part of the park.

NOTES:

PASSPORT STAMPS

JOHNSONVILLE STATE HISTORIC PARK

COUNTY: HUMPHREYS   **ESTABLISHED:** 1971   **AREA (AC/HA):** 2,000 / 810

DATE VISITED: SPRING ☐ SUMMER ☐ FALL ☐ WINTER ☐

WEATHER: ☀ ☐ ⛅ ☐ 🌧 ☐ ❄ ☐ ⛈ ☐ 💨 ☐   **TEMP.:**

FEE(S):   **RATING:** ☆ ☆ ☆ ☆ ☆   **WILL I RETURN?** YES / NO

LODGING: **WHO I WENT WITH:**

DESCRIPTION:

The park commemorates the Battle of Johnsonville, which occurred in 1864 during the Civil War, and the historic town of Johnsonville, which was flooded by the creation of Kentucky Lake by the Tennessee Valley Authority in the 1940s. The park offers a variety of interpretive programs to the public throughout the year. These programs include guided tours, Junior Ranger camp, and a variety of living history programs such as the annual Battle of Johnsonville commemorative event held in early November. Additionally, on November 4, the anniversary of the Battle of Johnsonville, the Park Ranger leads a walking tour. The tour includes an interpretive lecture focusing on the Battle of Johnsonville and takes visitors to various areas of the park related to the historic Civil War battle of 1864. There is a woodland trail that provides a look at several species of birds, including gulls, waders, woodpeckers, and white-breasted nuthatches. And sometimes even bald eagles. The park also offers great recreational opportunities for those who simply enjoy being outdoors. About 10 miles of well-maintained trails wind through this historic area and are enjoyed by hikers and recreational walkers alike. In addition to hiking and walking, bird watching, geocaching, swimming, shore fishing and picnicking are popular among park visitors.

PASSPORT STAMPS

JUSTIN P. WILSON CUMBERLAND TRAIL STATE PARK

COUNTY: ANDERSON, BLEDSOE, CAMPBELL, CLAIBORNE, CUMBERLAND, HAMILTON, MARION, MORGAN, RHEA, SCOTT, SEQUATCHIE   **ESTABLISHED:** 1998   **AREA (AC/HA):** 31,500 / 12,700

DATE VISITED: SPRING ☐   SUMMER ☐   FALL ☐   WINTER ☐

WEATHER: ☀ ☐   ☁ ☐   🌧 ☐   ❄ ☐   ⛈ ☐   🌬 ☐   **TEMP.:**

FEE(S):   **RATING:** ☆ ☆ ☆ ☆ ☆   **WILL I RETURN?** YES / NO

LODGING: **WHO I WENT WITH:**

DESCRIPTION:

It is the first linear park in Tennessee, crossing 11 Tennessee counties. The park is a scenic hiking trail. It became the 53rd state park in the state of Tennessee. In 2002, the park was renamed for Justin P. Wilson in honor of his work to help make the Cumberland Trail vision a reality. Wilson served as deputy governor of Tennessee from 1996 to 2003. The Cumberland Trail follows a line of pristine high ridges and deep ravines that lie along the Cumberland Plateau. The trail is designed for hikers as a sustainable, one-way hiking trail that is part of the Great Eastern Trail through the more remote areas of the Appalachian Mountains.

NOTES:

PASSPORT STAMPS

LONG HUNTER STATE PARK

COUNTY: DAVIDSON   **ESTABLISHED:** 1974   **AREA (AC/HA):** 2,600 / 1,100

DATE VISITED: SPRING ☐ SUMMER ☐ FALL ☐ WINTER ☐

WEATHER: ☀ ☐ ⛅ ☐ 🌧 ☐ ❄ ☐ ⛈ ☐ 🌬 ☐   **TEMP.:**

FEE(S):   **RATING:** ☆ ☆ ☆ ☆ ☆   **WILL I RETURN?** YES / NO

LODGING: **WHO I WENT WITH:**

DESCRIPTION:

The park is located primarily along the eastern shores of Percy Priest Lake. The park offers a variety of recreational activities, including fishing and hiking, and has two boat launch ramps on J. Percy Priest Lake, a group camp, backcountry campground, conference center and visitor center. More than 20 miles of hiking trails provide a variety of terrain and habitats. The park also manages Sellars Farm, a state archaeological site near Lebanon to the east. Sellars Farm is one of the few Native American mounds in Tennessee that is protected under government ownership. Based on artifacts discovered at Sellars Farm, the community appears to have been occupied during the Mississippian Period around 900 AD until about 1500 AD. There's a short loop trail around the farm which is a good hike for guests with children and offers a unique learning experience.

NOTES:

PASSPORT STAMPS

MEEMAN-SHELBY FOREST STATE PARK

COUNTY: SHELBY **ESTABLISHED:** 1944 **AREA (AC/HA):** 12,539 / 5,074

DATE VISITED: SPRING ☐ SUMMER ☐ FALL ☐ WINTER ☐

WEATHER: ☀️☐ ☁️☐ 🌧️☐ ❄️☐ ⛈️☐ 🌬️☐ **TEMP.:**

FEE(S): **RATING:** ☆ ☆ ☆ ☆ ☆ **WILL I RETURN?** YES / NO

LODGING: **WHO I WENT WITH:**

DESCRIPTION:

The park borders the Mississippi River and includes two lakes - Poplar Tree Lake and Lake Piersol. There are many camping opportunities throughout the park. Deer, turkeys, otters, beavers, foxes and red lynx are throughout the forest. More than 200 species of songbirds, waterfowl, shorebirds and birds of prey can be seen, including the American bald eagle. This area is a favorite of bird watchers. Meeman-Shelby Forest offers more than 30 miles of hiking trails that wind throughout the park. Visitors interested in hiking will enjoy the approximately 8-mile, wooded Chickasaw Bluff Trail. It is open to hikers and meanders along the bluffs with the largest loop overlooking Poplar Tree Lake. The park is home to one of the largest and most beautiful golf courses in the Southeast. The 36-hole wooded course is divided into two 18-hole courses.

NOTES:

PASSPORT STAMPS

MONTGOMERY BELL STATE PARK

COUNTY: DICKSON   **ESTABLISHED:** 1943   **AREA (AC/HA):** 3,782 / 1,531

DATE VISITED: SPRING ☐   SUMMER ☐   FALL ☐   WINTER ☐

WEATHER: ☀ ☐   ☁ ☐   🌧 ☐   ❄ ☐   ⛈ ☐   🌬 ☐   **TEMP.:**

FEE(S):   **RATING:** ☆ ☆ ☆ ☆ ☆   **WILL I RETURN?**   YES / NO

LODGING: **WHO I WENT WITH:**

DESCRIPTION:
The park serves as a natural oasis for local residents and a peaceful retreat for travelers. The park is home to three lakes and provides visitors with the opportunity to enjoy the sun on the shores of the beach and paddle on the calm waters. The park was once the center of the iron industry in Middle Tennessee. The park's namesake, Montgomery Bell, established one of the largest iron industries in Tennessee. Iron was once considered more valuable than gold and was a very lucrative industry at the time. There are many activities you can try at the park. Primarily these include hiking, biking, golfing and fishing. There are nearly 19 miles of trails throughout the park, one of which runs along the perimeter of the park. Paddle boats and kayaks are available for rent.

NOTES:

PASSPORT STAMPS

MOUSETAIL LANDING STATE PARK

COUNTY: PERRY **ESTABLISHED:** 1986 **AREA (AC/HA):** 1,247 / 505

DATE VISITED: SPRING ☐ SUMMER ☐ FALL ☐ WINTER ☐

WEATHER: ☀️☐ ☁️☐ 🌧️☐ ❄️☐ ⛈️☐ 🌬️☐ **TEMP.:**

FEE(S): **RATING:** ☆ ☆ ☆ ☆ ☆ **WILL I RETURN?** YES / NO

LODGING: **WHO I WENT WITH:**

DESCRIPTION:

The park is located on the east bank of the Tennessee River. The most popular attraction is fishing. Along the banks you can fish for perch, bream, crappie, striped bass, and catfish. The park has one daytime trail, a 3-mile trail. There is also one night trail, an 8-mile trail with two covered shelters. Tradition has it that a fire broke out in one of the area's tanneries, where oak trees were used to tan hides, which forced the mice in the tannery to flee. This exodus of mice contributed to the naming of the area Mousetail Landing, and the park got its quirky name from this fiery event.

NOTES:

PASSPORT STAMPS

NATCHEZ TRACE STATE PARK

COUNTY: HENDERSON **ESTABLISHED:** 1955 **AREA (AC/HA):** 10,154 / 4,109

DATE VISITED: _____ SPRING ☐ SUMMER ☐ FALL ☐ WINTER ☐

WEATHER: ☀ ☐ ⛅ ☐ 🌧 ☐ ❄ ☐ ⛈ ☐ 🌬 ☐ **TEMP.:** _____

FEE(S): _____ **RATING:** ☆ ☆ ☆ ☆ ☆ **WILL I RETURN?** YES / NO

LODGING: _____ **WHO I WENT WITH:** _____

DESCRIPTION:
Surrounded by breathtaking views of the Tennessee River, Natchez Trace State Park is a nature lover's paradise. Hiking trails in the park range from half a mile to 4.5 miles, and there is also a 40-mile overnight trail. The trails wind through forests and fields and along the banks of Natchez Park's lakes and streams. Visitors can also enjoy the museum, which offers local and park history, picnic facilities, camping, and boating. The park offers activities for visitors of all ages. Fishing is a favorite activity, and anglers can choose from four lakes. The park has cabins, a group lodge, campgrounds, picnic areas, playgrounds, a soccer field, a regulation shooting range.

NOTES:

PASSPORT STAMPS

NATHAN BEDFORD FORREST STATE PARK

COUNTY: BENTON   ESTABLISHED: 1929   AREA (AC/HA): 2,587 / 1,047

DATE VISITED: SPRING ☐   SUMMER ☐   FALL ☐   WINTER ☐

WEATHER: ☀️☐ ⛅☐ 🌧️☐ ❄️☐ ⛈️☐ 💨☐   TEMP.:

FEE(S):   RATING: ☆ ☆ ☆ ☆ ☆   WILL I RETURN?   YES / NO

LODGING: WHO I WENT WITH:

DESCRIPTION:

The park was named in honor of Confederate cavalry leader, General Nathan Bedford Forrest. Despite his controversial figure, Forrest is remembered by some as a renowned Civil War military tactician. More than 30 miles of hiking trails offer short trips or longer hikes. Two backcountry shelters are available for overnight hikes, which can be reserved with a permit issued at the park office. The park is located on Kentucky Lake, where fishing is very popular. There are commercial marinas and public boat launches nearby. Fishermen can catch smallmouth bass, largemouth bass and striped bass, sauger, crappie, bream and catfish. The Tennessee River Folklife Museum is located atop Pilot Knob at the end of State Route 191. The museum interprets the life and customs of people living along the lower Tennessee River in the late 19th and early 20th centuries.

NOTES:

PASSPORT STAMPS

NORRIS DAM STATE PARK

COUNTY: ANDERSON, CAMPBELL **ESTABLISHED:** 1953 **AREA (AC/HA):** 4,038 / 1,634

DATE VISITED: SPRING ☐ SUMMER ☐ FALL ☐ WINTER ☐

WEATHER: ☀☐ ☁☐ 🌧☐ ❄☐ ⛈☐ 🌬☐ **TEMP.:**

FEE(S): **RATING:** ☆☆☆☆☆ **WILL I RETURN?** YES / NO

LODGING: **WHO I WENT WITH:**

DESCRIPTION:

The park is located on Norris Reservoir. With over 800 miles of shoreline, the park offers recreational boating, skiing and fishing. The park has a fully equipped marina with a boat ramp open to the general public. Houseboats and pontoon boats are available for rent along with other types of boats. Both the east and west portions of the park have several miles of short hiking trails that wind through the forest on the slopes of the ridge and along the lakeshore. Hiking trails also cross the TVA-controlled small wilderness area of the Bluff River west of the dam. The Lenoir Museum Cultural Complex includes the Lenoir Museum and two historic structures- the Rice Gristmill and the Crosby Threshing Barn. Nearby attractions include the Museum of Appalachia. A Smithsonian affiliate, the museum portrays an authentic mountain farm and pioneer village and offers cultural and historical exhibits.

NOTES:

PASSPORT STAMPS

OLD STONE FORT STATE ARCHAEOLOGICAL PARK

COUNTY: COFFEE **ESTABLISHED:** 1973 **AREA (AC/HA):** 776 / 314

DATE VISITED: SPRING ☐ SUMMER ☐ FALL ☐ WINTER ☐

WEATHER: ☀️☐ ☁️☐ 🌧️☐ ❄️☐ ⛈️☐ 💨☐ **TEMP.:**

FEE(S): **RATING:** ☆ ☆ ☆ ☆ ☆ **WILL I RETURN?** YES / NO

LODGING: **WHO I WENT WITH:**

DESCRIPTION:

Native Americans used the area continuously for about 500 years, eventually leaving it abandoned. The park is named after the stone structure used by European settlers who came to the area hundreds of years after the Native Americans abandoned it. The main hiking trail runs along the wall of the Old Stone Fort, which was used by Native Americans as a ceremonial gathering place. In addition to exploring the remains of the stone fort by hiking the trails, you can see the magnificent waterfalls in the area and enjoy the beauty of nature. Many trails wind through this scenic park, along with trail markers that provide information about the history of the area. The park also allows RV camping. The campground is located near the Duck River, which meanders throughout the park. In addition to hiking, campers can spend the day fishing or bird watching.

NOTES:

PASSPORT STAMPS

PANTHER CREEK STATE PARK

COUNTY: HAMBLEN **ESTABLISHED:** 1967 **AREA (AC/HA):** 1,444 / 584

DATE VISITED: SPRING ☐ SUMMER ☐ FALL ☐ WINTER ☐

WEATHER: ☀☐ ⛅☐ 🌧☐ ❄☐ ⛈☐ 🌬☐ **TEMP.:**

FEE(S): **RATING:** ☆ ☆ ☆ ☆ ☆ **WILL I RETURN?** YES / NO

LODGING: **WHO I WENT WITH:**

DESCRIPTION:
The park is located on Cherokee Reservoir in the historic Holston River Valley, 6 miles west of Morristown. The park offers access to a variety of recreational activities such as paddling (canoeing, kayaking and paddleboarding), golf, hiking, boating, biking, fishing, bird watching and horseback riding. The park has 17 different hiking trails covering over 30 miles of terrain at all levels of difficulty. There are also over 15 miles of mountain biking trails ranging from easy to difficult. Cherokee Lake provides year-round fishing for bass, crappie, bluegill, catfish, rockfish and bream. Nearby commercial marinas provide boat launches and rentals.

NOTES:

PASSPORT STAMPS

PARIS LANDING STATE PARK

COUNTY: HENRY **ESTABLISHED:** 1945 **AREA (AC/HA):** 841 / 340

DATE VISITED: SPRING ☐ SUMMER ☐ FALL ☐ WINTER ☐

WEATHER: ☀️☐ ☁️☐ 🌧☐ ❄️☐ ⛈☐ 💨☐ **TEMP.:**

FEE(S): **RATING:** ☆ ☆ ☆ ☆ ☆ **WILL I RETURN?** YES / NO

LODGING: **WHO I WENT WITH:**

DESCRIPTION:
Park is located on the western shore of the Tennessee River, which is dammed to form Kentucky Lake. The park sits on the widest part of the lake making it the perfect location for all water sports such as fishing, boating, swimming, and waterskiing. The park also offers a beautiful and challenging, 18-hole golf course. The park is named in honor of an old steamboat and freight landing on the Tennessee River. In the 19th century, the river landing was an important delivery point for goods to service settlements in the region and a shipping point for agricultural products. Deer, turkey, fox and coyotes can be seen in the area. Eagles are often seen during the winter months.

NOTES:

PASSPORT STAMPS

PICKETT CCC MEMORIAL STATE PARK

COUNTY: PICKETT   **ESTABLISHED:** 1942   **AREA (AC/HA):** 19,200 / 7,800

DATE VISITED: SPRING ☐   SUMMER ☐   FALL ☐   WINTER ☐

WEATHER: ☀️☐ ☁️☐ 🌧️☐ ❄️☐ ⛈️☐ 🌬️☐   **TEMP.:**

FEE(S):   **RATING:** ☆ ☆ ☆ ☆ ☆   **WILL I RETURN?** YES / NO

LODGING: **WHO I WENT WITH:**

DESCRIPTION:
The park is located northeast of the Town of Jamestown and is adjacent to the Big South Fork River and Recreation Area. It features wildlife including caves, natural bridges and other rock formations. The park offers boating, camping, lodging, hiking and many other activities. In 2015, the park earned the International Dark Sky Park silver level designation. It became the first state park in the Southeast to earn this prestigious recognition. Visitors can enjoy expansive, rich views of the night sky similar to those found in many western states. The Pickett CCC Museum contains exhibits and interpretive artifacts depicting the Civilian Conservation Corps' contributions to Tennessee's parks and natural areas. More than 58 miles of hiking trails wind through the wilderness of Pickett State Park and the surrounding forest. They vary in length and difficulty, from short one-day trails suitable for families to longer multi-day backpacking trails.

NOTES:

PASSPORT STAMPS

PICKWICK LANDING STATE PARK

COUNTY: HARDIN **ESTABLISHED:** 1969 **AREA (AC/HA):** 681 / 276

DATE VISITED: SPRING ☐ SUMMER ☐ FALL ☐ WINTER ☐

WEATHER: ☀☐ ☁☐ 🌧☐ ❄☐ ⛈☐ 🌬☐ **TEMP.:**

FEE(S): **RATING:** ☆ ☆ ☆ ☆ ☆ **WILL I RETURN?** YES / NO

LODGING: **WHO I WENT WITH:**

DESCRIPTION:
The park is located around the damming of Pickwick Lake on the Tennessee River and is named for Pickwick Landing, a 19th century riverboat stop. Known for its excellent water recreation, the lake and river offer fishing, boating, swimming and a marina. In addition to water sports, guests can enjoy golfing, bird watching, picnicking, nature walks and tennis. The park also offers three public beaches for swimming. Circle Beach and Sandy Beach are located in the day-use area of the park, and a third is located across the lake in the Bruton Branch primitive area. In total, there are approximately two miles of public swimming beach in Pickwick. There are campgrounds within the park.

NOTES:

PASSPORT STAMPS

PINSON MOUNDS STATE ARCHAEOLOGICAL PARK

COUNTY: MADISON **ESTABLISHED:** 1966 **AREA (AC/HA):** 1,200 / 490

DATE VISITED: SPRING ☐ SUMMER ☐ FALL ☐ WINTER ☐

WEATHER: ☀☐ ⛅☐ 🌧☐ ❄☐ ⛈☐ 🌬☐ **TEMP.:**

FEE(S): **RATING:** ☆ ☆ ☆ ☆ **WILL I RETURN?** YES / NO

LODGING: **WHO I WENT WITH:**

DESCRIPTION:
The park contains at least 15 Native American mounds. In addition to Saul Mound, the group includes Ozier Mound, Twin Mounds, and Mound 31. Archaeological evidence suggests that the mounds were intended for both burial and ceremony. The Pinson Mounds museum is designed to replicate a Native American mound. The building includes 4,500 square feet of exhibit space, an archaeological library, a theater and 'Discovery Room' for historical exploration. Outdoor attractions at Pinson Mounds State Park include hiking trails that provide access to Native American mounds and picnic facilities.

NOTES:

PASSPORT STAMPS

PORT ROYAL STATE PARK

COUNTY: MONTGOMERY, ROBERTSON **ESTABLISHED:** 1978 **AREA (AC/HA):** 26 / 11

DATE VISITED: SPRING ☐ SUMMER ☐ FALL ☐ WINTER ☐

WEATHER: ☀☐ ⛅☐ 🌧☐ ❄☐ 🍃☐ 🌬☐ **TEMP.:**

FEE(S): **RATING:** ☆☆☆☆☆ **WILL I RETURN?** YES / NO

LODGING: **WHO I WENT WITH:**

DESCRIPTION:
The Red River runs through the center of the park, and the covered bridge at Port Royal once crossed it. The park was established to preserve the elements of early Tennessee history, namely settlement and early transportation, as well as the heritage of the Trail of Tears. The day use only park offers hiking, picnicking, kayaking, fishing and interpretive lectures upon request. Within the park are the remains of several old roadbeds, one of which dates back to prehistoric times. In addition to roads and bridges, as you walk through the park you will see the remains of foundations of stores, houses and warehouses, some of which date back to the 18th century.

NOTES:

PASSPORT STAMPS

RADNOR LAKE STATE PARK & NATURAL AREA

COUNTY: DAVIDSON **ESTABLISHED:** 1973 **AREA (AC/HA):** 1,368 / 554

DATE VISITED: SPRING ☐ SUMMER ☐ FALL ☐ WINTER ☐

WEATHER: ☀️☐ ☁️☐ 🌧️☐ ❄️☐ ⛈️☐ 💨☐ **TEMP.:**

FEE(S): **RATING:** ☆ ☆ ☆ ☆ ☆ **WILL I RETURN?** YES / NO

LODGING: **WHO I WENT WITH:**

DESCRIPTION:

It is unique for its variety of wildlife viewing opportunities, environmental education programs, and hiking opportunities. The park has several miles of hiking trails of varying difficulty. It is designated for day use only. The park is an ideal place for nature lovers to observe owls, herons and waterfowl, as well as many species of amphibians, reptiles and mammals such as mink and otters. Hundreds of species of field flowers, mosses, fungi, ferns and other plants, as well as trees, shrubs and vines contribute to the area's natural ecological diversity.

NOTES:

PASSPORT STAMPS

RED CLAY STATE PARK

COUNTY: BRADLEY   **ESTABLISHED:** 1979   **AREA (AC/HA):** 263 / 106

DATE VISITED: SPRING ☐   SUMMER ☐   FALL ☐   WINTER ☐

WEATHER: ☀☐ ☁☐ 🌧☐ ❄☐ ⛈☐ 🌬☐   **TEMP.:**

FEE(S):   **RATING:** ☆ ☆ ☆ ☆ ☆   **WILL I RETURN?** YES / NO

LODGING: **WHO I WENT WITH:**

DESCRIPTION:

The park encompasses narrow valleys formerly used as cotton land and pasture. The park area was the last seat of the Cherokee Nation government before the U.S. military imposed the Indian Removal Act of 1830 in 1838, forcing most of the Cherokee people in the area to migrate west. The park is home to a natural landmark, Blue Hole Spring, which arises from beneath a limestone ledge to form a deep pool that flows into Mill Creek, a tributary of the Conasauga and Coosa River system. Blue Hole Spring, also known as the Council Spring, was considered sacred place to the Cherokee. The spring was used by the Cherokee for their water supply during council meetings. The park has an amphitheater that can accommodate up to 500 people. There are three trails in the park: the Connector Trail, the Blue Hole Trail, and the Council of Trees Trail, which are 0.15 miles, 0.2 miles, and 1.7 miles long, respectively.

NOTES:

PASSPORT STAMPS

REELFOOT LAKE STATE PARK

COUNTY: LAKE, OBION   **ESTABLISHED:** 1965   **AREA (AC/HA):** 280 / 110

DATE VISITED: SPRING ☐ SUMMER ☐ FALL ☐ WINTER ☐

WEATHER: ☀️☐ ⛅☐ 🌧️☐ ❄️☐ ⛈️☐ 🌬️☐ **TEMP.:**

FEE(S):   **RATING:** ☆ ☆ ☆ ☆ ☆   **WILL I RETURN?** YES / NO

LODGING: **WHO I WENT WITH:**

DESCRIPTION:
The park is located in the northwest corner of Tennessee and is famous for fishing, boating and wildlife viewing. The lake was formed by a series of violent earthquakes in 1811-1812 that caused the Mississippi River to recede for a short time, creating Reelfoot Lake. Reelfoot Lake is a flooded forest. While Majestic Cypress trees rise above the water, there are many submerged cypress stumps below the surface. The lake is home to nearly all species of shorebirds and wading birds, as well as bald eagles and American bald eagles. It also has a diversity of turtles and snakes. Deep marsh kayak tours are offered in March and April, and scenic pontoon boat tours are offered from May through September. Although the shallow lake offers many boating and fishing opportunities, swimming is not permitted in the lake. There are several hiking trails in the park that are popular for bird watching and wildlife observation. There are campgrounds in Reelfoot Lake State Park. Activities at the park include boating, fishing, hiking, museums and a nature center, picnic facilities, wildlife viewing, and scheduled programs and events.

NOTES:

PASSPORT STAMPS

ROAN MOUNTAIN STATE PARK

COUNTY: CARTER   **ESTABLISHED:** 1959   **AREA (AC/HA):** 2,006 / 812

DATE VISITED: SPRING ☐   SUMMER ☐   FALL ☐   WINTER ☐

WEATHER: ☀ ☐   ☁ ☐   🌧 ☐   ❄ ☐   ⛈ ☐   🌬 ☐   **TEMP.:**

FEE(S):   **RATING:** ☆ ☆ ☆ ☆ ☆   **WILL I RETURN?** YES / NO

LODGING: **WHO I WENT WITH:**

DESCRIPTION:

The park includes rich hardwood forest along rugged ridges. Visitors can hike along streams and ridges, visit the century-old Miller Farm, or go cross-country skiing during the winter months. There are approximately 12 miles of hiking trails and 2.25 miles of mountain bike trails. Levels of difficulty range from easy to strenuous. Fishing is a popular activity in the park. The Doe River is cool enough year-round to be home to three species of trout. Brook trout, as well as rainbow and brook trout, are stocked regularly. There are campgrounds within the park. Visitors will find themselves surrounded by all kinds of wildlife, from black bears to box turtles, white-tailed deer to wild turkeys and ospreys to owls roaming the park.

NOTES:

PASSPORT STAMPS

ROCK ISLAND STATE PARK

COUNTY: WARREN, WHITE **ESTABLISHED:** 1969 **AREA (AC/HA):** 883 / 357

DATE VISITED: SPRING ☐ SUMMER ☐ FALL ☐ WINTER ☐

WEATHER: ☀☐ ⛅☐ 🌧☐ ❄☐ ⛈☐ 🌬☐ **TEMP.:**

FEE(S): **RATING:** ☆ ☆ ☆ ☆ ☆ **WILL I RETURN?** YES / NO

LODGING: **WHO I WENT WITH:**

DESCRIPTION:
The park is located on the upper reaches of Center Hill Lake at the confluence of the Caney Fork, Collins and Rocky Rivers. The rugged beauty of the park includes the Caney Fork Gorge below Great Falls Dam. These views are some of the most scenic and significant in the East Hill. Great Falls is a 10-foot cascading horseshoe-shaped waterfall located below a 19th-century cotton textile factory that it fed over 100 years ago. The Caney Fork River Gorge offers scenic vistas, waterfalls, deep pools and limestone trails ideal for hiking, swimming, fishing, kayaking and sightseeing. It also has a natural sandy beach and boat access on Center Hill Lake. There are campgrounds in the park. Hiking trails include two trails that lead to the north and south shores of Great Falls Gorge, and a 3-mile trail that follows the Collins River. Deer, woodpeckers, and wildflowers are common sites along the park's trails.

NOTES:

PASSPORT STAMPS

ROCKY FORK STATE PARK

COUNTY: UNICOI   **ESTABLISHED:** 2012   **AREA (AC/HA):** 2,036 / 824

DATE VISITED: SPRING ☐   SUMMER ☐   FALL ☐   WINTER ☐

WEATHER: ☀︎☐ ⛅︎☐ 🌧☐ 🌨☐ ⛈☐ 🌬☐   **TEMP.:**

FEE(S):   **RATING:** ☆ ☆ ☆ ☆ ☆   **WILL I RETURN?** YES / NO

LODGING: **WHO I WENT WITH:**

DESCRIPTION:

The park is adjacent to the Cherokee National Forest and is in close proximity to the Appalachian Trail. Hiking and mountain biking are allowed on a network of old roads, and fishing is permitted in Rocky Fork and South Indian Creeks. The steep, rugged terrain is drained by numerous cool mountain streams including its namesake, Rocky Fork Creek, which flows through the park. The stream is located in the pristine Rocky Fork watershed. With large moss-covered boulders, deep pools, and eddies the cold, fast flowing stream is noted for miles of excellent native trout fishing. A variety of fungi thrive in Rocky Fork's cool, moist climate. The lush forest is home to many federally listed animal species, including the world's fastest aviator, peregrine falcon, yonahlossee salamander and jumping wood mouse. The Black Bear also makes its home here. The park is part of the Unicoi Bear Reserve. If hiking in the forest, it is recommended that hikers be familiar with the area and have experience navigating the backcountry using GPS, compass and maps.

NOTES:

PASSPORT STAMPS

SEVEN ISLANDS STATE BIRDING PARK

COUNTY: KNOX **ESTABLISHED:** 2013 **AREA (AC/HA):** 425 / 172

DATE VISITED: SPRING ☐ SUMMER ☐ FALL ☐ WINTER ☐

WEATHER: ☀︎☐ ☁︎☐ ☂︎☐ ❄︎☐ ⛈︎☐ 🌬︎☐ **TEMP.:**

FEE(S): **RATING:** ☆ ☆ ☆ ☆ ☆ **WILL I RETURN?** YES / NO

LODGING: **WHO I WENT WITH:**

DESCRIPTION:
The diverse natural landscape of aquatic and grassland habitats makes the park a prime birdwatching site, with over 190 species of birds observed. Songbirds, hawks and waterfowl can be seen along the meadow trails, and several old barns are a favorite refuge for fawns. The park encompasses land along the French Broad River in Knox County, about 19 miles east of Knoxville. This peninsula offers more than 8 miles of natural trails, rolling hills and views of the Smoky Mountains. The park also offers biking and fishing. Fishing is available on the French Broad River. There are kayak launches in the park.

NOTES:

PASSPORT STAMPS

SGT. ALVIN C. YORK STATE HISTORIC PARK

COUNTY: FENTRESS **ESTABLISHED:** 1967 **AREA (AC/HA):** 295 / 119

DATE VISITED: SPRING ☐ SUMMER ☐ FALL ☐ WINTER ☐

WEATHER: ☀️☐ ⛅☐ 🌧️☐ ❄️☐ ⛈️☐ 🌬️☐ **TEMP.:**

FEE(S): **RATING:** ☆ ☆ ☆ ☆ ☆ **WILL I RETURN?** YES / NO

LODGING: **WHO I WENT WITH:**

DESCRIPTION:

The park is located nine miles north of Jamestown in Pall Mall, Tennessee and pays tribute to one of the most successful soldiers of World War I. The visitor center includes historic store displays modeled after Sgt. York's General Store, houses an exhibit with World War I artifacts, and offers interpretive displays about Sgt. York. The park includes a farm and mill that once belonged to the soldier. Along with the millhouse and milldam, the park includes York's two-story house, York's general store and post office, the Wolf River Cemetery (where York and his family are buried), the Wolf River Methodist Church, the York Bible Institute, and various picnic facilities.

NOTES:

PASSPORT STAMPS

SOUTH CUMBERLAND STATE PARK

COUNTY: SEQUATCHIE GRUNDY, FRANKLIN, MARION, **ESTABLISHED:** 1978 **AREA (AC/HA):** 30,899 / 12,504

DATE VISITED: **SPRING** ☐ **SUMMER** ☐ **FALL** ☐ **WINTER** ☐

WEATHER: ☀ ☐ ⛅ ☐ 🌧 ☐ ❄ ☐ ⛈ ☐ 🌬 ☐ **TEMP.:**

FEE(S): **RATING:** ☆ ☆ ☆ ☆ ☆ **WILL I RETURN?** YES / NO

LODGING: **WHO I WENT WITH:**

DESCRIPTION:
The park offers some of the best hiking and backcountry camping in the region. Twelve trails provide access to most parts of the park, which protects a number of unique ecosystems on the escarpments and canyons of the southern Cumberland Plateau. There are more than a dozen large waterfalls in the park, the highest of which is Foster Falls in Marion County. The park contains both natural and historic treasures, as well as 90 miles of hiking trails. Although the park consists of nine separate areas spread over several counties, it is managed as one park. The Fiery Gizzard Trail is a 12.5-mile one-way trail that connects Grundy Forest and Foster Falls. Hikers can observe nature, swim in Fiery Gizzard Creek, and view spectacular rock formations, cascading streams, waterfalls, rocky gorges, panoramic views and lush forests. The rock formations make this park ideal for rock climbing and abseiling. Caves and historic ruins can be found throughout the park along with waterfalls and wildlife.

NOTES:

PASSPORT STAMPS

STANDING STONE STATE PARK

COUNTY: OVERTON　　　**ESTABLISHED:** 1939　　　**AREA (AC/HA):** 855 / 346

DATE VISITED:　　　　　　　　　SPRING ☐　SUMMER ☐　FALL ☐　WINTER ☐

WEATHER: ☀☐　☁☐　🌧☐　❄☐　⛈☐　🌬☐　**TEMP.:**

FEE(S):　　　**RATING:** ☆ ☆ ☆ ☆ ☆　　　**WILL I RETURN?** YES / NO

LODGING:　　　　　　　**WHO I WENT WITH:**

DESCRIPTION:

The park is located in the Standing Stone State Forest on the Cumberland Plateau. The park takes its name from Standing Stone, a 12-foot tall rock standing upright on a sandstone shelf that was said to have been used as a boundary line between two Indian nations. When the rock fell, the Indians placed a portion of it on an improvised monument to preserve it. The stone is still preserved in nearby Monterey. The park has over 8 miles of day hiking trails. The 69-acre Kelly Lake (also known as Standing Stone Lake) is popular for fishing, with black bass, catfish, trout and bluegill being the most well-known species. Boating is also fun for park visitors, and you can even rent boats here. If you want to swim, the park also has a pool that is open seasonally or you can swim with the fish in Kelly Lake, Mill Creek or Morgan Creek.

NOTES:

PASSPORT STAMPS

SYCAMORE SHOALS STATE HISTORIC AREA

COUNTY: CARTER **ESTABLISHED:** 1975 **AREA (AC/HA):** 70 / 28

DATE VISITED: SPRING ☐ SUMMER ☐ FALL ☐ WINTER ☐

WEATHER: ☀ ☐ ☁ ☐ 🌧 ☐ ❄ ☐ ⛈ ☐ 🌬 ☐ **TEMP.:**

FEE(S): **RATING:** ☆ ☆ ☆ ☆ ☆ **WILL I RETURN?** YES / NO

LODGING: **WHO I WENT WITH:**

DESCRIPTION:
The park protects an area where several important historical events took place that occurred in the late 1800s. Leaving the English colonies, settlers began arriving along the old Watauga fields in search of a new life on Cherokee lands. John Carter, one of the major political, military and business leaders of that era, and his son Landon, built a house called the Carter Mansion, three miles from Sycamore Shoals. This structure is the oldest standing frame house in Tennessee and dates from the mid to late 1770s. Fort Watauga was built in 1776 to protect settlers from Cherokee attack. The 1.20 mile long Patriot Trail is located on the south bank of the Watauga River. The trail features interpretive signs describing historical events in the area.

NOTES:

PASSPORT STAMPS

TIMS FORD STATE PARK

COUNTY: FRANKLIN **ESTABLISHED:** 1978 **AREA (AC/HA):** 2,200 / 890

DATE VISITED: SPRING ☐ SUMMER ☐ FALL ☐ WINTER ☐

WEATHER: ☀️☐ ⛅☐ 🌧️☐ ❄️☐ ⛈️☐ 🌬️☐ **TEMP.:**

FEE(S): **RATING:** ☆ ☆ ☆ ☆ ☆ **WILL I RETURN?** YES / NO

LODGING: **WHO I WENT WITH:**

DESCRIPTION:

The park is located in the shadow of the Cumberland Plateau in south-central Tennessee. Tims Ford Lake is considered one of the most scenic lakes in Tennessee and is considered one of the best lakes for fishing and recreation in the Southeast. Located within the park, Lake View Marina offers pontoon boat rentals as well as a boat launch and marina. Boating, kayaking, canoeing and fishing are just some of the many water sports available to visiting vacationers. The park offers many lodging options. There are campgrounds in the park for tent or RV vacationers. Another popular activity is golfing. The park offers scenic lake views and over 30 miles of hiking and biking trails.

NOTES:

PASSPORT STAMPS

T. O. FULLER STATE PARK

COUNTY: SHELBY **ESTABLISHED:** 1938 **AREA (AC/HA):** 1,138 / 461

DATE VISITED: SPRING ☐ SUMMER ☐ FALL ☐ WINTER ☐

WEATHER: ☀☐ ⛅☐ 🌧☐ ❄☐ ⛈☐ 🌬☐ **TEMP.:**

FEE(S): **RATING:** ☆ ☆ ☆ ☆ ☆ **WILL I RETURN?** YES / NO

LODGING: **WHO I WENT WITH:**

DESCRIPTION:

The park is historically significant. Named after a very influential African American of the time, Dr. Thomas O. Fuller, who spent his life empowering and educating African Americans. Park attractions include picnic areas, tennis courts, a swimming pool (Olympic size), basketball courts, a softball field, 6 miles of hiking trails, and campgrounds. The park is a place that protects and showcases unique natural habitats while offering a wide variety of outdoor recreational facilities. The park's nature center is open during the summer and offers exhibits and natural history programs. Hiking trails range from moderate to difficult.

NOTES:

PASSPORT STAMPS

WARRIORS' PATH STATE PARK

COUNTY: SULLIVAN   **ESTABLISHED:** 1952   **AREA (AC/HA):** 950 / 380

DATE VISITED: SPRING ☐   SUMMER ☐   FALL ☐   WINTER ☐

WEATHER: ☀ ☐   ⛅ ☐   🌧 ☐   ❄ ☐   ⛈ ☐   🌬 ☐   **TEMP.:**

FEE(S):   **RATING:** ☆ ☆ ☆ ☆ ☆   **WILL I RETURN?** YES / NO

LODGING: **WHO I WENT WITH:**

DESCRIPTION:
Warriors' Path State Park was named for the Great Cherokee War and Trading Path. The park is located on the banks of Patrick Henry Reservoir on the Holston River. The park is home to boating and fishing activities, hiking trails, a world-renowned bike trail system (which is a designated National Recreation Trail), an award-winning nature education program and a nationally recognized golf course. The park offers a variety of hiking, biking, and horseback riding trails. The hiking trails run through forests and wetlands and range from paved, accessible trails to challenging climbs. There are also over 8 miles of bike trails. Horseback riding trails are available for both independent riders and those interested in guided walks. The marina at Patrick Henry Reservoir offers slips and kayak and paddleboat rentals. Several public ramps are available for visitors. Typical fish in the lake include crappie, trout, catfish, bream and perch. There are many picnic tables in the park. There is an 18-hole golf course on the shores of Lake Patrick Henry.

NOTES:

PASSPORT STAMPS

PHOTOS   **PARK NAME**..

PHOTOS   PARK NAME……………………………………………………………………

PHOTOS   **PARK NAME**..

PHOTOS   PARK NAME……………………………………………………………………………

PHOTOS   PARK NAME..

PHOTOS   PARK NAME..

PHOTOS   **PARK NAME**..

PHOTOS   PARK NAME..

PHOTOS   **PARK NAME**..

PHOTOS   PARK NAME..

Thank you for taking the time to read my book. I hope you found it enjoyable.

Your feedback is important to me, and I would greatly appreciate it if you could take a moment to share your thoughts by leaving an online review.

Your review will not only help me improve as an author but also assist other potential readers in making informed decisions.

Once again, thank you for your support and for considering leaving a review.

Warm regards,

Max Kukis Galgan

Write to me if you think I should improve anything in my book:

maxkukisgalgan@gmail.com

SEE OTHER BOOKS

COLORADO STATE PARKS BUCKET LIST	FLORIDA STATE PARKS BUCKET LIST	GEORGIA STATE PARKS BUCKET LIST
IDAHO STATE PARKS BUCKET LIST	INDIANA STATE PARKS BUCKET LIST	KANSAS STATE PARKS BUCKET LIST
MAINE STATE PARKS BUCKET LIST	MICHIGAN STATE PARKS BUCKET LIST	MINNESOTA STATE PARKS BUCKET LIST

MISSOURI	NEW YORK	OHIO
OREGON	PENNSYLVANIA	TENNESSEE
TEXAS	UTAH	VIRGINIA

WASHINGTON
STATE PARKS
BUCKET LIST

WISCONSIN
STATE PARKS
BUCKET LIST

Made in United States
Orlando, FL
19 February 2025